GRIEF

SONGS

JACK FOLEY

Sagging
Shorts

Set in Williams Caslon with LaTeX.

ISBN: 978-1-944697-48-8 (paperback)
ISBN: 978-1-944697-49-5 (ebook)
Library of Congress Control Number: 2017945081

Sagging Meniscus Press
web: http://www.saggingmeniscus.com/
email: info@saggingmeniscus.com

For Adelle

What you want is not the expressive but something that liberates you from the need for the expressive.

—August 22, 2016

From my book, RIVERRUN, *in scripto continua:*

```
asweagewediscovertoourdismaythatrelationshipsw
ehadexpectedtolastalifetimedisappear:lovedones
,eventhemarvelousones,die.inanageofskepticism,
inwhichtheheavenstoriescarrylittleweight,howdo
wedealwiththisimmenselydisturbingsituation,thi
sblowtoallouregotism?
```

I told Adelle, through tears, that I wished with all my heart that the news had been given to me. She said she would have felt the same way.

—June 5, 2016

GRIEF SONGS

November 13, November 18

I think that, recently, neither
of us
remembered
the date
of our first
meeting
but it was preserved
in a cartoon:
November 18, 1960.
Today,
I sat
in an ice cream shop
with my friends
Paul and Vu
and Vu's daughter Kaitlin.
I fell silent
uncertain whether
the date were today, November 13
or the next Friday, November 18.
The 18th won out
but I had to wait
until the sweetness and good humor
of my friends had ended.
We parted, smiling.

But tears poured out of me
as soon as I was alone.
I suddenly remembered
the moment when Adelle and I first tongue kissed
in a "date parlor"
in Towson, Maryland
(*November 18*)
and I began to feel
the love
that will stay with me
till the end of my days

PERHAPS IT'S BEST to begin with Dellwackia. For many years, Adelle and I drew cartoons for each other. We were the only people who saw them. The central figures were a king, Jack Wack (me—"J.W.") and a queen, Dell Dell (a name Adelle's father used to call her), but there were many others including Jack Wack Dog and Dell Dell Dog; Young Lioness and her mate; Salvador Dully (the tiny sun—not small because he was distant but small because he was small); Looney (the moon); Iacchus Wacchus, the Roman, with his mate, Della Della Puella Bella; Dr. Quack with his nurse, Flowence Nightindell (whenever anyone falls ill, Dr. Quack is sent on an all-expense-paid trip to someplace else: everyone likes him, but no one wants him tending the sick—though no one really gets sick in Dellwackia); etc. They inhabited a country named for the queen and king: Dellwackia. Everything—rocks, trees, everything—in Dellwackia talked. The figures had voices which Adelle and I provided, and they became an everyday fixture of our life. There was never a day in which, at various times, we didn't speak in the voices to one another. When I told Adelle I had an appointment with the podiatrist, she immediately said, "Jack Wack Dog needs to have his toenails clipped!"

Jack Wack and Dell Dell were comic, parodic, child-like, but they were also possessed of the pure love that children sometimes manifest: "Daddy!" "Mommy!" If at times something went wrong with Jack and Adelle, nothing ever went wrong with them. They believed in what they called "LLLLAAAAAHHHHVVVEEE." And we could become them whenever we wished. When, in her last days, Adelle apologized to me for being "gwumpy"—which she wasn't, she was brave and loving and intelligent— she did so in the voice of Dell Dell. (Like some children, Dellwackians pronounced their r's as w's, sometimes as h's, though there was one instance in which they pronounced a w as an r: the famous pulp fiction character, The Shadow became in Dellwackia "The ShadoR." As a Dellwackian, of course, he didn't "know" very much. He regularly forgot to put eye holes in his mask so that, though he could be seen, he couldn't see anyone else.)

It depressed me enormously to think that that whole world we had created would simply vanish with Adelle's death, so I took a look at the cartoons we had saved. I was surprised to find that they were better than I thought: some of them had enormous energy. (At one point we were doing them every day.) It occurred to me that they might even be made public. At least that way they would have some staying power. I should add that they were begun and worked on long before I had any fame as a poet—I was nothing more than a graduate student at UC Berkeley—and, again, they were originally meant for no one's eyes but Adelle's and mine.

The cartoons, like the choruses we were to perform many years later, were an instance of call and response.

Poet Jake Berry writes of them,

> Something that comes through in these images is how young you were. You are living your life together while preparing for life. A sense of struggle, of confronting the unknown. Dellwackia is a strange new land where one must toil in order to make one's fortune. Many hours of your days you are torn from one another in order to make a future together unfold. The humor reveals, and conceals, uncertainty. This is a wonderfully illustrated, tender, affectionate prelude to the life you would live together. All of this comes through so clearly in the image of Young Wack headed on down the road while Dell Dell waves goodbye and good luck. Time was not lost on you. Nothing has been wasted. Life preciously tended in cartoons between young lovers.

❇

Wednesday, June 15, 2016, 12 days before her death, 10 days before her lapsing into a coma from which she never awoke, Adelle wrote in the voice of her cartoon character, Dell Dell:

> "SOWWY
> Nous toutes don't mean to be gwumpy.
> We LLLLAAAHHHVVVEEESSS
> tous les gars
> Who are generous and loving and v stwessed."

Later, on the phone, she asked me whether I forgave her: "Does forgive?" Yes.

"Nous toutes"—"all of us" (female)—and "tous les gars"—"all the guys"—are references to a song by the great French singer/songwriter, Georges Brassens, "Brave Margot." It is a song Adelle and I both loved, and we adapted the phrases to the Dellwackians.

I think that what Adelle meant by "gwumpiness" was the fact that she felt constantly depressed about what was happening to her—as who wouldn't? She wanted me to know that she wasn't blaming me. Brave Adelle! Anatole Broyard writes of "the aloneness of the critically ill, a solitude as haunting as a Chirico painting" ("The Patient Examines the Doctor").

On June 16, Father's Day, she felt sad that she hadn't gotten anything for me. Though I knew she had a significant tremor in her writing hand, I asked her to make me a cartoon. She did. There are lines that betray the presence of the tremor, but the figure comes through loud and clear: Dell Dell is saying, "love, love, love."

✸

the life we made
was a charm against death
but death found a way into it
my love my dear love

. . .

Before We Knew…

May 2016

as we are now
    here we are
not at some future
    on this late may
time at this
    day
moment
    you who are never
as we deal with
    sick
all the
    are suddenly
particularities
    taken
of
    with something
the moment
    and need
as we are now
    attention
listen
    fear

to the moment
grips me
as it
and the lack
constantly
of knowledge
fails
prayer is not
as it
an option
constantly
we maintain
rises
as best we can
and
our rituals
falls

Before Her Death...

Matthew Fox writes, "One of the most wonderful concepts that Hildegard [von Bingen] gifts us with is a term that I have never found in any other theologian... the word *viriditas* or greening power" (*Illuminations of Hildegard of Bingen*). The word suggests "veritas," truth, as well as "veridicus," speaking the truth. *Wikipedia*: "The definition of viriditas or 'greenness' is an earthly expression of the heavenly in an integrity that overcomes dualisms. This greenness or power of life appears frequently in Hildegard's works."

Some years ago, *Poetry Flash* editor Joyce Jenkins challenged me to "write a nature poem" for her Watershed event. I found my mind returning to Kore / Persephone, especially to her aspect as seed, thrust underground but emerging to flower. I remembered as well W.C. Williams' poem, "Of Asphodel, That Greeny Flower" and Denise Levertov's book of nature poems, *The Life Around Us*. Adelle was diagnosed with cancer on Saturday, June 4, 2016. I told her doctor, "We want to keep her." Adelle chimed in, "I want to be kept." The doctor remarked that Adelle was "taking the news well." She then asked, "What about *him*?"—me. Adelle answered, accurately, "A little less well."

In 1960—we were both twenty—she sang an ancient French song, "A la Claire Fontaine," to me. It was a sweet gesture of young love. The refrain of the song is "Il y a longtemps que je t'aime / Jamais je ne t'oublierai" ("I have loved you for a long time / I will never forget you"). Over the years we often sang the song together. In 2016 I sang the song to her as she lay dying in the hospital: "I have loved you for a long time / I will never forget you." She died at 5 a.m. on June 27, 2016.

I wrote many years ago:

> It's not a dream
> We lose those we love
> but we love
> anyway

I read "Viriditas" to Adelle shortly before her death.

Viriditas

Viriditas—
the dream
of a green
world

It is not
enough
to say
"the life around us"—
we *are*
"the life around us"

it is not possible
to be
apart
from
nature
("*natura naturans*")

    the conditions
    in which
    consciousness—
    "this"

consciousness—
happens
are serious, tentative, and limited
this dream
of green

I *am* that flower
you hold
in your
hand

we are
light
coming to consciousness
of
itself
men & women
of light

what is mind
but light?
what is body?

"Make LIGHT of it,"
writes my friend
James
Broughton—

Walking,
I vanish into light—

      Kora—the seed—
      above ground—under—
          the need
      to follow her—down the rabbit hole
            following the
    idea
    of resurrection—
      seed-
  time vanishes/returns   we grow
  in branch and root
  in winged or finny stuff
  or cloven hoof
  in bird-
  sound, animal alarm or
  pleasure
  (describe a scene—
  scene vanishes—
  mind appears—)

Kore   woman
under
ground
        No need
that is not satisfied

of food

or sex—

. . .

    greenness, love:
    as you lie in this moment
    of danger,
    as you sleep
    wondering if the next sleep
    will be death,
    "this greeny flower,"
    this green
    comes to you
    the power of life
    Viriditas

My Wife Adelle's Death

What you discover in such a situation
is what Rousseau called
le néant des choses humaines
the nothingness of human affairs
Adelle's concerns—the laundry, our finances,
her plants, dinner, people at AC Transit, people
in the local community, poetry people, whether
I parked the car close enough to the curb,
her VISA card, the Toyota, her haiku, the goldfish, me,
the light in the leaves as she passed by in the morning,
credit cards, J.R.R. Tolkien, Octavia Butler, *Miss Fisher's Murder
Mysteries*, the egrets at Lake Merritt,
the homeless on her way to AC Transit
(to whom she gave money and boxes of raisins),
her son and daughter in law,
hundreds of others
in a complex web of caring—
all disappeared poof in a few moments
on the afternoon of June 25, 2016
in a Kaiser hospital room
when she fainted in "septic shock" and her dear heart stopped.
Suddenly, all of that was gone
as if it never existed
le néant des choses humaines

I remember it, some of it—even most of it—but for her
it's a spider web someone brushed off a window—
gone.
It is this that we make poems and stories and beautiful lies
to avoid:
this sudden view
when a long-loved, long-known, long-accepted person dies
& we see it
deep and clear

For Maw Shein Win, Who Lost Her Sister

How do you come back to life
When someone close to you
Someone who *is* you—
A wife, a sister—
Is suddenly gone.
"Don't forget to bring the dearth certificate,"
A friend accidentally wrote:
He called it, accurately, a dearth, an absence, a loss
But it is more than that:
It is a diminution
That draws us into its darkness.
The struggle of the other's dearth
Is also the knowledge of our own
Our own diminishment
Until we wish to be the
Nothing
Our loved one has become: smoke, vapor.
When my wife died,
I walked through my kitchen
Weeping
And saying, "I want to die."
I know she would have never wished that for me
And yet
The strength of death—its lure—

Was that strong.
Our love, our happy life together
Brought to a sudden end—
My wife, your sister.
Why do ghosts
Rattle chains and frighten strangers?
Let them return
To where they will be loved and appreciated.
Let them live in our hearts.
Look: the house still has your scent in it;
Your clothing hangs in the closet!
Dear Maw,
Let us both
Try to bear the unbearable,
Try to live
In a world which has taken the dearest thing to us
And destroyed it, though we knew
From the beginning that that was possible,
That death was the price of life.
But we know it now
In a way that is different from what we knew.

Spoken at Adelle's Funeral

grief
like a leaf

fallen on me

July 17, 2016

For Adelle

> The one who looked after me has gone
> The one I looked after has gone
>
> —Bertolt Brecht, *Love Songs*

How do you mourn the absence of someone you've seen almost every day of your life and whose daily presence was always a comfort to you? We've all seen children in the midst of what seems to us to be some more or less trivial setback begin to howl and weep in utter despair and anguish. We learn to contain that childish impulse as we grow, but in an event like this, the child returns with a vengeance, and you experience what seems to be endless and bottomless sorrow.

Adelle and me. People came and went, but from the beginning there was love and a commitment to one another—a desire to promote each other, to help each other. That deep commitment was understood and held to by both of us, no matter what else happened. When I entered the poetry world, I never presented myself as "Jack Foley": it was always "Jack and Adelle Foley"— though organizers often had trouble with that billing. My first book was called *Letters/ Lights—Words for Adelle.* It was accompanied by a cassette tape on which she performed.

Adelle was diagnosed with cancer on June 4; she died on June 27. During that short time I tried to be her caregiver, cooking, comforting, helping in any way I could. I was rather overwhelmed with things to do—things for Adelle (many trips to Kaiser), household things, things for the radio show. I wrote when I could but Adelle was the center of everything.

We often felt very close to one another even in the midst of this ordeal. At one point she apologized for being "grumpy" and asked whether I forgave her. I forgave her. She was in fact wonderful throughout: intelligent, brave, and loving. At times we spoke or interacted and she was just as she always was: momentarily it was as if this crisis wasn't real. But there were other times when she was sick: "queasy," unable to eat, fatigued. We kept up our rituals as well as we could.

I know she's dead, but I also know that as long as I am alive, she will be alive. And if my work lives, she will live in it. And I know that her own work will be intertwined with mine. I am putting together another book of her haiku; it is tentatively titled, *Early the Next Day*. There are many beautiful poems that have not yet seen the light. I had hoped to edit the book with her, but that wasn't possible. She writes in "Peaceful Walk,"

> The water lapping
> Against the stone barrier
> The sun on my face

I wrote, "how can there be sunlight, and you not in it."

※

I'd like to conclude these opening remarks with a poem. I've written several poems to Adelle over the years. This one was written for our 40th wedding anniversary, fifteen years ago. She told me she kept it with her at AC Transit and looked at it from time to time.

Forty Times for Forty Years:
An Anniversary Poem for my Wife, Adelle

each line a speaking of her name

Forty years? what are they? dust
memories
"I think I'll get married," someone said
when I was young, "it'd be a cool way to spend a year"
It wasn't, for her.
Forty years. Who is married that long
except someone's parents?—
a couple cordial enough
but hardly real.
If I remember,
you are always there
except for my very earliest life
I have a friend
with no marital history

no history of "relationships":
he remains in rapt wonder before his childhood
My own history
is a violent severance
of the child—
and then you
You held your hands out to me before I knew the need
Without knowing, you kept my imagination
clear and in the world
You gave me a son
who has grown
into a loving intelligent man
No one can tell my life
without telling yours
No one can say my name
without adding yours as well
What are the throbbing intricate ways of love?
We barely know, nor should we
It flings us here and there
It opens us.
In all this clamor,
in the rubble of my affections and my grief
I say your name, "Adelle"
and say it
forty times
for forty years.

✳

RECENTLY, THERE HAVE been many poems and expressions of grief for Adelle. This one is from poet John Oliver Simon:

691 — Adelle 2 — The Viewing

Adelle in her coffin with copper bracelet
that will be found encircling her ulna
by raccoon archaelogists way downstream
who may be able to reconstruct her face

with its smart mouth now pulled quiet forever
but will never awaken its quick laughter
Jack's in endless freefall of bottomless grief
no hug from compadres can hope to console

raccoons will little note nor long remember
his grief, their lifetime love, the poetry scene
around the San Francisco Bay Area

at the turn of our second millenium
but let them say this: she lies there dead who was
in life a faithful and practical artist.

for Adelle Foley (1940 – 2016)

I wrote between the lines of John's poem:

691 — Adelle 2 — The Viewing

Adelle in her coffin with copper bracelet
    I saw her
that will be found encircling her ulna
    (Leo, lioness:
by raccoon archaelogists way downstream
    August 15th)
who may be able to reconstruct her face
    as she moved towards

with its smart mouth now pulled quiet forever
    the flames
but will never awaken its quick laughter
    that will forever
Jack's in endless freefall of bottomless grief
    transform her.
no hug from compadres can hope to console
    I had kissed

raccoons will little note nor long remember
    my fingers
his grief, their lifetime love, the poetry scene
    and touched

around the San Francisco Bay Area

> *her lips*

at the turn of our second millennium

> *my love*

but let them say this: she lies there dead who was

> *of over fifty*

in life a faithful and practical artist.

> *years*

***

ADELLE'S BODY was cremated this morning.

I was speaking to Thomas Marsden, Funeral Arranger and Licensed Embalmer at Chapel of the Chimes, where I had brought Adelle's body. I heard something in his speech.

"Are you from Boston?"

"Yes."

"Boston Irish?"

"Yes."

He knows all about George M. Cohan and was delighted when I mentioned him. He spoke of the Cagney film, *Yankee Doodle Dandy*, and told me that Freud said the Irish were the only race that could not be psychoanalyzed: they were too crazy. Went into a brogue as he told me stories of things his "mither" said. "Call me Tommy," he said. I told him that my father worked for Cohan as a tap dancer and told many stories. ("Cohan was blondie. When he got mad, he threw chairs around.") It was a somewhat amazing connection—one Adelle would have loved. She too knew all about Cohan, through me. Marsden said, "She was treated like a queen," and I think that was true.

It helped a great deal.

I was with her (her body) for a while and spoke to her and wept. You viewed the preparations for cremation from the other side of a window. You pressed the button that opened the crematorium door. You saw the intense flame and the box as it moved toward it. Then Tommy motioned and I pressed the button to close the door.

Adelle had looked fine in the coffin—"like a queen"—but it was a right-side, three-quarter view. As she was about to go into the flame I saw her face a last time, as did Sean. It was the left side. The morticians hadn't worked on that, and it bore the marks of the hospital.

> This road:
> with no man traveling on it,
> autumn darkness falls.
>
> (Literally: *This / road / : / going-person / be-none /*
> *[with] / autumn-nightfall*)
>
> —Basho (Harold G. Henderson translation)

July 18, 2016

＊

A FRIEND FROM MALAYSIA sent me a poem about being "blessed." This is how I answered him:

Dear Ismail,

Thank you for the poem!

I have been blessed in many ways too. Adelle and I had love and respect for one another throughout our lifetime. Yet love is greedy and always wishes more. The depth of the love is the depth of the sorrow that comes rushing in when the relationship is suddenly ended. I was foolish, but it never occurred to me until very recently that she might die. She was never sick—never until she contracted this vicious, vicious cancer. Our lives were so intertwined—on a daily basis—that it seemed impossible for that relationship to end. So when it did, I was unprepared. All I could think to do was to give her life in any way I could, by writing about her, by publishing her writing, by making tributes to her—by presenting her to the world as what she was: a wonderfully talented, brilliant, loving woman who by some miracle loved me her whole life long.

What you feel at such a moment is a seemingly bottomless sorrow, something that has no end. I know there will be a way out of it—and I know I *need* to find a way out of it—but at the moment it's difficult to imagine what that way out could possibly be.

I think I am slowly returning to life, but it seems that with each step towards the living there is a counter step towards the dead.

Today is July 27. Adelle died on June 27. The term is not "anniversary"—which means the turning of a year—but "mensiversary," the turning of a month.

I went to the store and bought a new pair of shoes, a new belt, and a shirt whose color attracted me.

But I also spent a fair amount of the day weeping.

Writing is a help and has been a help throughout this entire process of seeing Adelle through her death—and then the days after her death. My ability to write, to "speak" in this way, has kept me together.

I wrote a birthday poem for a young woman who will be performing with me. She is a singer, so she understands breath and the intricacies of vowels and consonants. Perhaps we will do the poem together—with the two voices coming together and separating. Her name is "Helen," which rhymes a little with "melody," which is how I got the opening lines. *La cancion* is Spanish and means "the song."

Helen—

Helen

Melody—

Melody

Music to
        Music to
Hear &
        Hear &
See
        See
Marvels
        Marvels
Come forth
        Come forth
In jazz
        In jazz
Buzz-biz
        Buzz-biz
Or lyrical
        Or lyrical
Magnaflights
        Magnaflights
Of Sonic
        Of Sonic
Ecstasy
        Ecstasy
Helen—
        Helen—
Melody—
        Melody—

She moves
She moves
In music
In music

By the river, just as the sun comes down and darkness is falling, you hear it, a sound that is simultaneously ancient and now, a woman sound, your mother, your lover, your sister, your friend, all in that voice, all saying, REJOICE, all loving, all moving, all sweetness & light, all crying out *la cancion*, which is itself a river, a flow, sweet air surrounding us as the music

sways
& plays

Helen—
Melody

The Loss

somewhere in the world
somewhere in the world
there wanders
there wanders
a shadowy figure
a shadowy figure
that was
that was
a portion of myself
a portion of myself
somewhere in the world
somewhere in the world
but not here
but not here
somewhere in the world
somewhere in the world
not here
not here

it is loose, poor *anima* poor womanworld wandering
in the foul byways and alleys,
the soiled streets
of the immense,

threatening
city

somewhere in the world
not here

[Part of what is lost is, in Jungian terms, the animus or anima figure, the masculine side of women, the feminine side of men. The loved one has been the embodiment of that figure for many years—so when we lose the loved one we also lose a portion of ourselves. We want the loved one back but we also want back that lost portion of ourselves. This is a passage addressed to Adelle from my poem, "Stanzas from Djerassi," written some years ago when I was living by myself at the Djerassi Foundation Artists Colony. It is echoed in the poem above:

you're walking in the kitchen now (not here)
you're fixing breakfast (not here)
you're sipping tea (not here)
reading (not here)
I am there (not here)
with you (not here)
thinking of you
here (not here)]

The House, the Urn

"The sun on my face"
—Adelle Foley

Everything here
Was for both of us
Not just for me
If it's just for me
It seems so—
I don't know what it means:
Everything empty
I put your urn
Near where you sat reading.
So many days
I'd come downstairs
And there you would be
Engrossed in a book
But willing to be interrupted
If I spoke
Or bent to kiss you
You knew what I meant
Always
I could read you a poem
Or tell you an idea
That had just occurred to me

You always listened
You always smiled
I know you would want me
To go on from your death
But, O, my love
O, my love—
The sun
Blesses your urn
Every morning
It cheers my heart, which
When you died,
Nearly (like yours) stopped beating.

Upon my 76th Birthday

Life
Comes crowding in on me
Presents, well wishes
From dear friends
From people I don't know
All in the shadow
Of the death of my dearest
Who would never have missed my birthday.
My love for her
Circles around the house
We shared for more than forty years.
She is still here
Even in her deep absence.
I have plans
For her birthday (6 days away)
Which our son has designated "a nice wake."
Thanks to the human hearts
Which have opened to me in my sorrow.
Life is forever changed
But, as everyone says to me, goes on.
I am writing choral pieces
Which do not replace but remember her.
I am working with a new person
Who respects the work

Adelle and I did for more than thirty years.
Death is a visitor to this wonderful birthday party
(As in a way he is to all birthday parties)
But life is here too
In the friends, the love, the presents
In the voices of my son and daughter in law
Who sang happy birthday to me
Moments after I awoke
To say hello to my 76 years
On this difficult, love-struck planet.
Thank you to all the visitors,
Even the shadowy one.
I welcome him too
Though it costs me my heart.

August 9, 2016

Poem by Adelle, Found This Morning of her Birthday in a Yellow Notepad

The wind swirls around
The pear tree. The branches bend
But they do not break.

I answered the poem:

I am sorely bent
In this terrible deathwatch:
Not yet did I break.

August 15, 2016

August 15, 2016

It's your birthday
My dear, dead love
I had begun a birthday poem
My wife
My life
And had already bought some gifts for you
A Monday—Moon Day
"Looney" in our Dellwackian fantasy
Who paired with the tiny sun,
"Salvador Dully"
You made a cartoon for me
Eight days before your death
(Six before the day
You forever lost consciousness)
I am trying to find
Another life to fit me
But what could ever fit me
So well as the life we made
As Moon and Sun
As Dell Dell and Jack Wack
As the EEE Monster
And the DDD Monster
As all the phantasmagoria
That rose out of our love,

That kept our love
Forever alive:
They never stopped loving
Even when you and I faltered
They wondered why Dellwackia
Suddenly looked
Like a hospital room.
I've cooked dinner for you tonight
Polpette, purpettes,
A meal you loved
That came from my mother's
Long Calabrese line.
Dear friends will join me
And then we'll watch
A favorite film:
Hitchcock's *Foreign Correspondent*
Looney and Salvador Dully
Will watch it too
And Dell Dell and Jack Wack
And the Monsters.
Everyone loves
The poems I've been writing
About your death
You were always my Muse
And today is the birthday
You could not celebrate.

Our love remains
In all these figures
In all these words
While you
Whirl through the universe
(If such things are true)
Forgetting birth and death
Forgetting Dellwackia and me
Remembering only
The deep configurations
Of Life and Love.

I added this note to the poem: The names mentioned are cartoon characters in a joint fantasy that Adelle and I maintained for years. We drew pictures for each other and gave the characters voices. She was Dell Dell—a name her father gave to her when she was a child. I, "J.W. Foley," was Jack Wack. The DDD Monster and the EEE Monster, etc. all figured into this fantasy, which took place in a country named for the queen and king: Dellwackia. We had a ritual for turning out the bedroom lights at night. The Dellwackians didn't understand electricity but they would all gather and in their various voices "blow out the candle." After the lights were out, I would say, "'Night, Dell." She would answer, "'Night, Wack." The lights are still on in our bedroom.

An Exchange With our Son, Sean

Jack:

Last night's birthday dinner for Adelle was a great success. Everyone loved everything. Pastina. Polpette. Everything. Paul brought wine. Rosetta made chocolate-dipped strawberries. But it left a barrage of dishes. Always great to see *Foreign Correspondent*. Adelle was toasted, read to, thought of. I didn't weep the whole night long. But I did (vehemently) this morning. It's as if a part of my body were gone. Phantom Wife Syndrome!

Sean:

I am happy the dinner was a great success but am sorry that the morning took a piece out of you. This is a process in which two steps forward will be followed by many steps back. It is not surprising you would have a reaction. It raises again the fundamental question you are dealing with—namely what do you do with all of those formerly "living" memories? Even the past takes on a very different form than it did BEFORE she died.

Jack:

The past: yes, it does. Sometimes if I think of her—of the way she looked—I can only think of photographs, which horrifies me and leads directly to meltdown. Happily, this is not always the case. I remember most vividly touching her during those last weeks. And holding her hand in the hospital.

Sean:

You are still in the trauma period and the memory part will—I suspect—smooth out over time. But forgetting is sadly natural, and photographs are there to keep us from forgetting.

Jack:

> "Jamais je ne t'oublierai"
> I will never forget you

So I sang to her.

＊

Jake Berry on the photograph of Adelle in the scarf at Maliki Restaurant: "For the first time since her death I see her and I do not feel an immediate sense of loss or mourning. I feel an immediate sense of her presence, ever and always welcome, and needed."

I answered:

> I wish I could share your sense of not feeling an immediate sense of loss or mourning. I hung up the photograph in the breakfast nook near her urn—and had a major meltdown. Suddenly I remembered the moment I took the photograph, her sitting across the table from me, just as she was in the photograph. It was as if the photograph made it possible for me to reach out and touch her again. All I had to do was hold out my hand. And I remembered holding her hand as she lay dying in the hospital—the exact feeling of her hand (and of the moment when it grew cold). A flood of tears. Starting again even as I write this. The photograph made her seem so real. And her expression was so tender and loving. It was as if I lost her again.

> I don't see any let up in these intense feelings—no five stages for me! (Though it's possible that I'm experiencing all the stages at once.)

*

I TOLD ANOTHER FRIEND the way I reacted to the photo. He wrote this:

> Dear Jack,
>
> This is as it should and must be, don't you think?
>
> Adelle dwells in you.
>
> She dwells in the hearts of all the rest of us who cared and care.
>
> Love,
>
> Al

I answered:

> Of course I'm grateful to those who care, but as to *should* and *must*, I can't tell you anything about them. *In the whirlwind*.
>
> Love,
>
> Jack

Letter to a Friend

I'm doing what I can ...

Tremendous number of things to be done—and my energy quotient shifts. Unhappiness is exhausting.

I'm making an effort.

Various worries surface, and I think fear is a factor. My desire for Adelle to be still in my life—which is considerable—is also a fear of the future and how I can function in it.

There are various legal problems which are worrisome and time-consuming. For some reason, Adelle didn't list me as a beneficiary on the AC Transit MassMutual account. Probably just an error on her part, but this very likely means Probate—which I have to do for another account as well. Probate for MassMutual means a much larger tax bite out of what I'm supposed to get. People are trying to find a way around this. I have a feeling they will fail: Adelle should have named me as beneficiary. My financial advisor said, "We'll sue"—but I think that was hyperbole. I also have to contact various accounts to let them know that Sean is my beneficiary. Have to figure out which accounts to contact, how to contact them, etc. The Probate process may take a long time.

I'm trying to keep the radio show going, but I'm not very interested at the moment in doing interviews with people—discussing their work. Too much happening in my own headpiece. So I have to find other things to do. I do think I'll return to interviewing but I need a break from it at the moment. A couple of people are coming to the house. I told them to bring some poems. I'm thinking of a conversation about poetry rather than a discussion of a new book. This way I don't have to read someone's book.

There is an immense amount of STUFF in the house. Adelle's clothing, possessions, books are one area. But there are also the immense piles of papers she amassed. There are probably some important things in these piles—including drafts of poems—but I will have to go through everything to find out.

Taxes loom. Sept. 15. My financial advisor seems good and helpful and she will accompany me to a CPA. She thinks my taxes are relatively straightforward, but they are far from straightforward to me.

I need a performance partner. When Adelle was alive, she and I were live forces in the poetry scene. With her death we have become something like legends. Someone on Facebook wrote, "I saw them in 1992!" I feel like a surviving Beatle. A friend, Helen Wendy Loo has been very enthusiastic about performing with me but she is very busy with her own career as a singer and may not be able to do that much. Also: I doubt that she'd be able to travel with me to perform, the way Adelle did. This means that performances in LA and New York (or anywhere) might be singles only—which is not what I want.

I have several meltdowns per day. Intense weeping, feeling that I can't / don't want to go on. I think of these as the lure of death—but they are very strong.

I am immensely lonely. Everything in the house is set up for two: now only one in the house.

I had this thought, which brought on a meltdown: *You can love her and love her and love her, but you can't save her.* I wanted so much to save Adelle. I knew I couldn't but I did what I could. She had had a very good experience at Kaiser, gaining strength through intravenous feeding. At home, however, she began to starve herself: foods she could eat became fewer and fewer. Constant nausea. Finally she was eating nothing but water and 7Up; if she threw up the water and 7Up, she drank Gator Aid to restore her electrolytes. I said, "You're starving yourself," so on June 24 I brought her back to Kaiser. This time—there is no other way to put it—Kaiser killed her. They wanted to give her a CAT Scan. I helped her drink the "contrast" that she vomited up and that caused the aspiration that caused her death. We were doing what the doctors wanted. I was proud of her that she was able to finish it. The situation was terrible, and it brought on a terrible dilemma. *There were no good choices.* It was obvious that I should bring her back to Kaiser—to help her. Yet that's what killed her. Had I not brought her back to Kaiser, she would probably have lived a little longer. And I so wanted her to live. Yet she would have suffered and died eventually anyway. My chiropractor thinks that she wouldn't have lived very long in any case. "With that kind of cancer," he told me, "things get speeded up." It's certainly true that the shift to her inability to eat anything but water, 7UP and Gator Aid was very quick. I had hoped that Kaiser would offer her some intravenous feeding, but they wished to find out whether there was gastrointestinal blockage first: hence the CAT Scan. She did in fact get through the CAT Scan without vomiting, but on her way to the next test, an Ultra Sound (because her legs were swollen), she vomited up the contrast. Some of it of went into her lungs, choking her. She fainted, her body went into Septic Shock, and her heart stopped. She was placed on Life Support for two more days but she never awakened from the coma she had entered. I watched over her, holding her hand and speaking to her. Some interns came in to look at her; one of them remarked, "She's been through a lot." Later, a doctor told me, "Some parts of her have already passed." She wore her wedding ring throughout her ordeal, as indeed she did all the time. It melted into her ashes when she was cremated. When I felt her hand become cold, I knew she was gone. I kissed my fingers and put them to her lips. People have called her death a "blessing." *But with such blessings, who needs disasters?*

> I have loved someone
> Long and deeply
> "You still love her"
> Yes, of course I do

But I also know
That such love is *now*
Love of the dead

And I will need
Something living
If I am not to die too.

∗

I WROTE THIS a couple of days ago:

August 23, 2016

Dearest,
> *Dearest,*

It's been nearly two months
> *It's been nearly two months*

Since your death.
> *Since your death.*

People tell me
> *People tell me*

It gets better
> *It gets better*

With time.
> *With time.*

But it hasn't gotten
> *But it hasn't gotten*

Better.
> *Better.*

Your clothes still hang
> *Your clothes still hang*

Where you left them;
> *Where you left them;*

The blue robe

The blue robe

Is still where you tossed it

Is still where you tossed it

When we went to the hospital;

When we went to the hospital;

Your car

Your car

Is parked where you always parked it.

Is parked where you always parked it.

My little game

My little game

Of pretending you're still alive

Of pretending you're still alive

Is exposed as the lie it is

Is exposed as the lie it is

At every moment.

At every moment.

Yet I keep

Yet I keep

Pretending

Pretending

And can't disturb

And can't disturb

What you left behind.

What you left behind.

I live amid
  I live amid
The numinous
  The numinous
Knowing
  Knowing
The falseness
  The falseness
Of this world I hold
  Of this world I hold
In Sacris,
  In Sacris,
Treasuring
  Treasuring
The fiction.
  The fiction.

…

We did everything together.
You died. Shouldn't I die too?

…

Dearest,
Not always at sunset but today
  Not always at sunset but today

at sunset especially

at sunset especially

when the stunning beauty of this California sky

when the stunning beauty of this California sky

outside our house strikes me, and I remember

outside our house strikes me, and I remember

how we spoke of the sky

how we spoke of the sky

of color, of "Looney"

of color, of "Looney"

Not always at sunset but today

Not always at sunset but today

especially when I think of you

especially when I think of you

next to me, and the sun descends

next to me, and the sun descends

in its tremendous daily arc

in its tremendous daily arc

and I think with all my heart that it is absolutely incomprehensible

and I think with all my heart that it is absolutely incomprehensible

that you are not

that you are not

alive

Grief

"Grief" for me seems to be a sort of nervous breakdown in which the forces of life and death play themselves out in the most intense fashion. Three or four attacks a day: meltdowns. You can do nothing but wail and weep. And then, it's over; I can go on with my "normal" life. Such forces (life vs. death) probably exist all the time in everyone—Freud speaks of a "death instinct"—but the experience of grief causes them to intensify to an extraordinary degree. A friend's perception that I'm living in two worlds seems accurate.

End of August, End of our Birth Month

you, two months dead
we didn't know
it would be the last time
we would see each other
neither of us knew:
it was only a procedure
something that might work
to make her feel a little better
didn't know that these
would be the last conscious words
she would ever hear from me
(squeezing her toes):
"I'll be back in an hour, honey.
See you then. Love you."

How DOES ONE get through the nervous breakdown of grief?

"The Sun on my Face" (Adelle Foley)

these branches reach
back into the world
greedy for light

Gabriel Rosenstock's translation of my poem into Irish:

síneann na géaga seo
ar ais isteach sa domhan
santach ar sholas

September 10, 2016

A tree. A beginning. Maxwell Park, Oakland. Planted Wednesday, Sept. 7. The note says, "FOR ADELLE: A CALIFORNIA BUCKEYE LOSING ITS LEAVES FOR WINTER." Gaining them back again soon.

Note: A living redwood seedling was also planted in the forests of the Santa Cruz Mountains in Adelle's memory via the Sempervirens Fund. This was through the generosity of Lucille Lang Day and her husband, Richard Levine.

Cartoon: "Young Wack Weturns to Dellwackia U."

Jack and Adelle in Berkeley on "Jack Foley Day," June 5, 2010.

To Joyce Jenkins, *September 13, 2016*:

The death of Adelle and of Mark Baldridge leave enormous gaps—in Watershed, in everything. It's kind and generous of people to offer consolation but we both know that consolation really doesn't work. Adelle is both present in everything I do, everywhere I go—she was always in the car with me!—*and* absent. The moment my mind moves towards her, it also remembers her loss. People say to me that I have many good memories to comfort me, but every good memory comes with the price tag: loss. Every good memory makes me lose her again. I am trying to think of her not as someone who died but as someone who lived. I think the publication of the cartoons we exchanged will help with that, but I don't know for certain. I am doing various "tributes" to her, but how do you do a tribute to someone who has been such a deep part of your life for so many years? I hope—and almost believe—that I gave her a good life, a life that stimulated her and was better than the life she would have had as, say, an economist. She always had an interest in art and literature. She discovered J.R.R. Tolkien long before he became a paperback sensation—I used to give her Tolkien in hardcover—and I am certain that she would not have written poetry had it not been for me. She recorded a statement about what it was like performing with me, and she says some lovely things in it. I'm happy to have it. The response to her death has shown how many people—and how many kinds of people—she touched in her life. Just yesterday a woman driving by stopped her car when she saw me. She told me she worked at AC Transit and had known Adelle: she said how kind she had been, how smart she was. The woman had probably never read a line of Adelle's poetry. And the California Buckeye planted in Maxwell Park testifies to her extraordinary involvement in the neighborhood, in neighborhood projects. She had great intelligence, but she also had great compassion. For my whole life long, Adelle made it possible for me to function as the kind of poet I am, and she believed in me as a poet when absolutely no one else did. I think she was happier about "Jack Foley Day" in Berkeley than I was because it justified the faith she had in me and because she knew that the day (June 5, 2010) honored her as much as it did me. I wish she could have seen the outpouring of feelings for her that has happened since her death. It is gratifying, and I am trying to accept it as it is—as a gesture of love for her—and not as still another reminder of her death. The lines I placed on her urn remain true:

> Il y a longtemps que je t'aime
> Jamais je ne t'oublierai
> I have loved you for a long time
> I will never forget you

Phone Call

I dialed your work number, wondering.
Your last message was still on the machine.
"You've reached Adelle Foley at AC Transit.
I will be out of the office indefinitely…."
Heartbreaking,
But it was sweet to hear your voice again:
We spoke so often on the phone.

"Looney"

I saw the moon tonight
We talked about the moon—
how close to full it was
How close to full our lives

September 13, 2016

In Café Leila

all these living voices
how strange they seem—
these living
you gone
today someone told me
I was "lost"—
you were the one
I would tell
about it.
I had never noticed
until now
how close
the words "lost"
and "ghost"

September 16, 2016

✻

the shape of the pillows
on your side of the bed—
who but you and me knew that?

＊

POET A.D. WINANS wrote to me,

Feel for you.
Nicely put.
Stay strong.
Speak to the tree.

＊

Two Adelle incidents. I went up to the Union 76 station to have them check the tire pressure—as I usually do when the car gives me a message. I had to tell the man there, Kashmir, that Adelle had died. He said, sincerely, "Oh, she was a lovely lady." A little later I was rinsing the car off on Brookdale Avenue. The next-door neighbor across the street, who is African American, didn't know Adelle had died. He saw her car and thought she might be on vacation. When I told him, he said, "Miss Adelle…?" I said, "Yes." He said, "She was the first person who welcomed me when I moved into the neighborhood."

September 16, 2016

MELTDOWNS ALREADY A FEATURE of the day—for various reasons. One: in the bathroom I looked at the toilet bowl and remembered how Adelle had to rush there to throw up. I cleaned up after her. I couldn't cry about it then but I can now. Life seems so bleak and sad and useless. I know that's just the meltdown talking, but it's a loud voice. My situation "really" isn't so bad. I have friends, money, projects. I have reasons to live. Yet sometimes everything seems like shifting sand: nothing can be grasped, held.

I'm trying to focus on Adelle's life rather than on her death. Why should only two months (May, June) blot out so many years? Because sometimes it seems as though it's the death, with its struggles and horror, that lasts. I am the only person who went through that with her. The problem isn't just grief, though grief is a large element. The process of seeing Adelle through her death, which took place both in our house and in the hospital, seems to have traumatized me, so that it intrudes itself upon just about anything I think about her: I relive her dying every day. The fact that much of the process took place in the house means that almost anything in the house can bring it to mind: the toilet into which she was sick, the couch on which she tried to sleep, the 7UP cans I bought for her when she could eat almost nothing else. Everything tends to turn into a recollection of her dying, to bring forth the process of the trauma. I'm trying to extricate myself from the trauma, but it is extremely difficult because the trauma also brings with it sweet recollections of her last moments of life, the very last moments when it was possible to be with her.

I felt that the little moon poem was positive, a step towards life. But I have paid for it dearly this morning.

September 14, 2016

Poet Ann Sherman sent me a little haiku for Adelle:

> oh that salty tears
> might keep the vivid sunset
> memories of Dell

Many tears followed.

※

"You say you cared for her opinion yet you argued with her if her opinion differed from yours."

"It was *because* I cared for her opinion that I argued with her. If I hadn't cared for her opinion, I would have let her think whatever she wished—which is how I respond to many people. I *don't* care what they think. With Adelle I cared, so I wished to show her that what I was doing was valid. She was my audience, and she was sometimes a skeptical audience. But audiences can be like that. You have to win them over. I knew immediately that she was not a foolish audience; she was an intelligent audience. I wanted her to see what I saw."

"And she did?"

"She did."

…

she was my witness
the one who could say
whether my acts were wise
or foolish
the one
who named me

✳

people wish
to hang onto
their egos
so that
when you ask them
to speak their poem
against another poem
and
the poems
collide
they fear
(rightly)
that they
are losing
control:
they are
losing
control…

Duotaire

I was playing Solitaire on the computer. I suddenly flashed on how, if Adelle were anywhere near I would say, "How about a hot game of Duotaire?" and she would join me and we would play together. *Duotaire*. I can't tell you how much I wish I could say such a thing again.

Missing You in Form

I am a man of sorrow not of joy
See the couples laughing in the street
Hear their whispers, intimate and sweet,
—As sweet as William Powell and Myrna Loy!
There's no companion near me as I eat
No one to hear the stories I repeat
No one to listen to my codicil.
The loneliness that took me as a boy
Returns in my old age and leaves me ill-
Suited to the world that ebbs and flows
(I am a scholar of these bitter woes).
I am a man of sorrow—not of joy.
I am a man of sorrow, not of joy.

The Dress

Your clothing in the closet:
knives piercing me.
The request was simple:
a dress you bought in Paris.
Your cousin wished a keepsake.
The light in your closet
had been out for years,
so I used a flashlight.
Suddenly the things you wore
danced before me:
I saw your form in all of them.
The sweater I bought
which you thought was "wrong" for you
until friends told you
how beautiful you looked in it;
the "Mexican" skirt.
All your things,
your beautiful things—
knives
piercing me

...

Your clothing in the closet:
knives piercing me.
My flashlight
in the dark:
Your things,
Your beautiful things—

Weekly Chores / Poem Space

It's a bit of a drag, the constant
  when I perform
return to these necessaries.
  poetry
They come round again too quickly.
  I find that the man
Come do me again. Life goes on,
  who drove safely to the reading
offering nothing but itself. They are not
  has disappeared:
release except in the sense that,
  I am in
once finished,
  poem space
their necessity subsides.
  where anything
Be patient, fish. Things will return
  can happen
to normal in a few minutes. Whirl
  I am alive,
in the washer, clothing. Soon you'll be dry.
  but I (and all that pertains to I)

  has disappeared

Found in a file: lines from a poem written in 2013 after the death of Lucille Lang Day's daughter, Liana:

Shadows touch our faces with darkness,
We barely look
And someone is gone.

...

And I think
How none of us can possibly be alone,
Of the dendritic quality every life has
How every life without exception reaches out to others,
Of how she stood
In the wake of life
Though death claimed her

...

It is our *bliss*
That allows us to work
Into the long nights and days,
To have children who will die
As we die (and perhaps before us)
To make poems and stories and music and pictures

Even as we slip
Into the nothingness which was our first and will be our last
        condition—
Even as the ancient syllogism tells us:
All women are mortal
Liana was a woman
But she lived her life
In love.

Flowers

Today I saw a woman
with a large bouquet of flowers
coming out of Trader Joe's.
I remembered that, every Monday,
Adelle brought such a bouquet
from Trader Joe's
to AC Transit
to brighten her desk.
One Monday,
miscalculating a left turn
towards a parking lot,
she totaled the car.
The accident was her fault,
and she had to phone me.
I hurried to the scene.
There she stood, entirely alone,
holding her flowers
in front of the wrecked car.
She looked utterly forlorn
and uncharacteristically waif-like.
I could not be angry at her.
I could feel nothing but love
and a desire to comfort
the beautiful lost thing before me,

the thing clutching her flowers.
Now that I have seen her through her death
and she is gone,
I remember that moment
as what might have been disaster and anger
but was instead
love

November 9, 2016, the day after Donald Trump was elected president

Doxa

You believe that thinking about a subject is the expression of an opinion. This is the doing of the various news media, all of which believe that thinking is the expression of an opinion.

Just because you say, "I think" before expressing your opinion, you believe that you are thinking.

But that is not thinking. That is just expressing an opinion.

But if that is not thinking, then what is thinking?

Thinking is the perception of relationships between disparate objects. Thinking is not the expression of an opinion—which is really nothing but the disclosure of ego—but the awareness of connection and disconnection, connection and disconnection.

Who but Freud would have seen a relationship between an ancient Greek play and the children's nursery? He was thinking when he saw that connection. Einstein was thinking when he wrote "E=MC^2."

In fact, many people who have opinions have never had the occasion to think. Nevertheless, they think they think. But, as Shakespeare might have had a character say, they think they think amiss.

But, alas, not thinking leaves a void, a hole in the spirit. It has to be filled with something. What do you suppose it's filled with?

Dreams?

Not dreams: the opinions of others. These opinions fill up the void, the lack, if a person fails to think.

You can see it very clearly in so many, so many. They are huge emptinesses needing something to make them believe they are full. Full of life, full of opinions. Nonetheless, they are empty. Sad to see them.

Doxa, the Greeks called it. Doxa. We have it in "indoctrination." And "paradox": "originally denoting a statement contrary to accepted opinion."

Doxa.

POET JACK HIRSCHMAN asked me to write "something incendiary" for his anthology, *Overthrowing Capitalism*. This is what I produced:

Signs of the Times

There are some men

> *Workers of the world, unite*
> *You have nothing to lose but your chains*

Who wish to pursue inaction
There are women who wish to return to the hearth

> *Workers of the world, unite*
> *You have nothing to lose but your chains*

There are men who hate
Who wish to stir up minorities against minorities

> *Workers of the world, unite*
> *You have nothing to lose but your chains*

There are men who wish to build walls
To divide countries and peoples from one another

> *Workers of the world, unite*
> *You have nothing to lose but your chains*

Oppression is so lonely
Oppression is darker than the darkest alleyway at dusk as the sun
    fades

Workers of the world, unite
You have nothing to lose but your chains

Oppression isolates us from our deepest impulses
Oppression opens the door to the dead, who come flocking in to
    take the jobs (and the women) of the living

Workers of the world, unite
You have nothing to lose but your chains

The white policeman is oppressed
The black man he murders is oppressed (and dead)
Drug dealers are oppressed, lawyers oppressed, girls oppressed,
    women oppressed
Boys oppressed, LGBT oppressed
The sleepy man who opens the door to the great hotel—oppressed

Workers of the world, unite
You have nothing to lose but your chains

They lie on the streets, they are mourned by their mothers
Oppression is dense, oppression is deep as water-world

Workers of the world, unite
You have nothing to lose but your chains

Oppression is the drug of the rich
Oppression is the sexual expression of the rich

Workers of the world, unite
You have nothing to lose but your chains

You don't have to be rich to be an oppressor
You don't have to be white to be an oppressor

Workers of the world, unite
You have nothing to lose but your chains

The man who takes his hand to his woman—oppresses
The woman who cheats to maintain her job—oppresses

Workers of the world, unite
You have nothing to lose but your chains

The university professor knows it, the janitor of your building
    knows it
The woman selling kreplach at the grocery store knows it
Actors in a successful TV series are oppressed—listen to their
    interviews
The "news" is oppressed
Pop stars are oppressed

Workers of the world, unite
You have nothing to lose but your chains

Oppression is lonely, it unites with nothing
Oppression is weary, ready to fall to the sidewalk as it stumbles
      with worn-out shoes on the hard pavement

What is there to lose? Nothing
What is there to change? Everything

BLOW UP EVERYTHING!

    Workers of the world, unite
    You have nothing to lose but your chains!

Mauvais Temps

In French it means
Bad weather
But it could also mean
Bad Time
We live in mauvais temps
Storms gather
Impossible to know
What dreadful weather
What storms
Will stun
What stones
Will fall upon us
Mauvais temps
Rain and hail
Pour out of the mouths
Of the reckless men and women
We call our leaders
Mauvais temps
Bad times
Fall upon us
How many of the good
Have perished
How many who wished to be good
Have discovered delight

In corruption

How many fires

Have gone out

How many of the corrupt

Have taken power

And used it

To defeat all hope

Mauvais temps

What historical violence

What bad time

Has fallen upon us

What rage

To answer it

Shall we march

Shall we write poems and articles

Shall we treasure

What sweetness we have

And use it

In the coming darkness

Shall we answer the storms

With voices that know

Another possibility

Shall we speak to the storm

Without becoming

Storms

Ourselves

Mauvais temps
Bad time
Bad weather

Poem for the Times, Perhaps

Solitaire
> *hearts*

involves
> *clubs*

the restoration
> *spades*

of
> *diamonds*

a proper
> *aces*

hierarchy
> *kings*

when
> *queens*

terrifying
> *knaves*

anarchy
> *then*

threatens:
> *the numbers:*

the cards
> *ten*

distributed
> *nine*

by
eight
chance
seven
("Le Hasard")
six
are random
five
indifferent
four
to human
three
thought:
two

it is only
through the act
of intellect
and the endless human perception
of
connections

that
aces
order
kings

is

    queens

restored

    knaves

    and

    we

    can

      breathe

Changes

There will be changes in the house, love
As there would have been had you lived
I can't keep everything exactly as it was
When you were alive
I have, for instance, finally tossed out that rickety metal table
That I painted black
There are other small modifications
But I can't bear to live in this house
Without tokens of you in it

I have thrown nothing of yours away
Everyone tells me I should do that
Some have offered to help
They say the words "Good Will"
But I can't bear it
I can't bear to live in this house
Without something of you in it—

Without remembering
The way the house was full
When you were alive

...

Liebe Nacht
Let me sleep
Without dreams
Without voices
Without anything
But the deep,
Deep
Dark

＊

On the lost side of heaven
where the angels fell…

…

The receptionist said, "How can I help you?"
"I'll give you a list."

…

His greatest madness was his belief that he was sane
His greatest madness was his insistence
that he saw
reality

…

Hymn to Satan

The grandeur of the wolf
is not a penumbra
nor is it wind
it is no less than the refulgence
of the shadow of an animal
wounded in the garden at night
while you weep
like a wounded animal in the garden.

—Leopoldo Maria Panero, trans. Arturo Mantecón

(my writing between the lines)

Hymn to Satan

The grandeur of the wolf
   In the bedroom
is not a penumbra
   a small light gleams
nor is it wind
   disturbed by no wind
it is no less than the refulgence
   it gathers the ghosts
of the shadow of an animal
   of the animals (ourselves)
wounded in the garden at night
   who said good night
while you weep
   & smiled
like a wounded animal in the garden.
   in the gathering dark

A Short Trip to Tennessee and Alabama, Mirror of a Trip Adelle and I Took, Sept. 2015

> At the Airport:
> flash of Adelle's presence
> as I stood
> in line

The hotel is the same one Adelle and I stayed in a little over a year ago. I remember the style of the room—the bed, the chair, the desk, etc. The rooms here must all look similar. I remember being in what might have been this room when Adelle and I were here.

There's a little tube of body lotion in my home bathroom. I found the same tube in the bathroom of the hotel. Adelle must have liked it and taken it home with her. I hadn't realized that it had come from the hotel.

I had wondered what my reaction to this mirror trip would be. The trip seems to be something of a half way house. It's true that Adelle and I spent time here together and that we did many of the things I am now doing alone. But she didn't *die* here, as she did in Oakland. I continue to miss her with all my heart—and there are meltdowns—but the experience is less intense here. The trip seems to be, in that sense, healing.

DELIGHTFUL THANKSGIVING DINNER with Sean, Kerry, and
Sean's colleague, Jasmin Hyunju Kwon. I wrote this poem after-
wards, back at the hotel. The poem has been set to music by the
multitalented Jake Berry.

Thanksgiving Night

Here I am in the Tennessee night
listening for the sounds of Tennessee
What tenderness accosts me
What power of remembering
Seeing
the trees of Tennessee
the leaves that have not fallen
in their tenacious clinging.
I would nest among
these brittle tender leaves
these roaring sights
these things
of Tennessee

…

Bama—
leaves!

…

In Imitation of Xu Zhimo

Leaving Tennessee
on a gray cold morning
work done here
accents singing—
disturbing nothing
leaving as quietly
as a leaf
falls

...

ON THE PLANE HOME: A passage in Nina Serrano's novel, *Nicaragua Way* has one character calling another her "sister poet." I remembered that Adelle referred to both Mary-Marcia Casoly and Clara Hsu as her sister poets and I began to weep. Had to close the book and fight back the tears.

Carol: December Again

Christmas is the gift
Christmas is the gift
Of the Christ child
Of the Christ child
To a Mankind
To a Mankind
Which has not been "good."
Which has not been "good."
Its accouterment
Its accouterment
The tree
The tree
Is Pagan
Is Pagan
But assimilated.
But assimilated.
All is magic
All is magic
Baptize the tree
Baptize the tree
And it is Christian too
And it is Christian too
I write this poem
I write this poem

This Christmas
This Christmas
Wish
Wish
To speak to the soul
To speak to the soul
Of my dear dead wife
Of my dear dead wife
Who loved Christmas
Who loved Christmas
Though I do not
Though I do not
Believe in souls.
Believe in souls.
I believe in the longing
I believe in the longing
That makes us human
That makes us human
And tells us
And tells us
Against all knowledge
Against all knowledge
That the world is good
That the world is good
That the dead live
That the dead live

as Present

Dalí Tarot cards
der
e future.

,
ard
ck.

e.
n tell
rd
next?
lid Dalí
l fall?
lid that artist
o grief?

cards fall
hanged man—

That we too will live forever
That we too will live forever
Despite the cross
Despite the cross
Despite the death
Despite the death
Despite the fabulous
Despite the fabulous
December
December
Lies
Lies

December 1, 2016

FACEBOOK: SEAN PUT UP a few photos of a view of Oakland/San Francisco in the morning. It is the beautiful view from Adelle's hospital room a few moments after her death. I commented, "Beauty tinged with sadness." And then, "Morning. Mourning." The time was 5 a.m. An empty sky. When he took the photographs he told me he wanted always to remember the day of her death. June 27. The day she fell into the awful coma was Saturday, June 25, six months to the day before Christmas.

...

Light comes pouring in the window on Shadowday.

A FRIEND SENT ME a Christmas card—the first of the year—via email. It sparked the "Carol." The change from November to December made me think of how much Adelle loved Christmas and how this would be a "tough Christmas" without her. I went into meltdown, missing her intensely.

I sit
With my
And won
About th
I sit
  And dea
  Death's
  In the d
  Chance
  Rules m
  Who ca
  What c
  Comes
  When
  Fail an
  When
  Come
  When,
      As
  As the
    th

Leaf
   he
By leaf
   can tell you

memories appear
like potholes in the streets
of Oakland

COVER TO COVER with Jack Foley

December 28, 3:00 p.m., KPFA 94.1 FM

On today's show Jack reads from his book, *Grief Songs*. The show begins,

My friend Ivan Argüelles writes,

> I alone listening
> for your voice
> in the torn leaf
> *trembling*
> in my hand

Today's show is an exercise in longing.

It's the end of the year, and it's been a difficult year on many fronts. For me, one of the most difficult of these was the death of my wife Adelle after nearly fifty-five years of marriage—fifty-five years of her being the primary and dearest person in my life. I can't say that our relationship was perfect, but it was always loving and mutually supportive. After fifty plus years we still liked and respected each other, and seeing her through her death was by far the hardest thing I have ever had to do in my life. The shock of it remains with me and will probably remain with me to the end of my days. Had the situation been reversed, had I had the cancer, I'm sure she would have felt the same way.

So this is the end of a year in which something else ended—something which had been in many ways (and still is) the foundation stone of my life. I felt like what Ezra Pound memorably described in *The Cantos*: "a blown husk that is finished"—though Pound was quick to add, "but the light sings eternal." Seeing my desolation, people were kind. I can't tell you how many people told me they loved me. People who didn't know me told me they loved me. People who didn't like me told me they loved me. Yet the one person whose love I treasured above all else was gone—taken not by the cancer itself but by a procedure meant to alleviate the symptoms of the cancer, the physical discomforts of a terminal disease.

Song—poetry—has been my answer to grief. I told someone recently, "I have nothing but words. But I have words."

I have a book. It's called *Grief Songs*, and it has a publisher, Sagging Meniscus Press, though every time I declare the book finished and hand it to someone, I write another poem. On today's show I'm going to read some poems from that book. I do not believe in God, heaven, hell, life after death, reincarnation—none of those things. But song is real and it can name the *longing* for God, heaven, hell, life after death, reincarnation. Today's show is an exercise in such longing. One friend remarked, "You've invented religion."

The Fire

how I wish I could tell you, dearest,
of the tragic fire in Oakland
of how some texted their parents
to tell them they loved them
and they were about to die
and how others were found
hugging each other in a last, fearful
gesture of love;
and how we would have done the same
we would have done the same

December 21, 2016

Today
    Today
We would have been married
    We would have been married
For fifty-five years.
    For fifty-five years.
A few people know.
    A few people know.   *the darkness of the night,*
No one
    No one   *the long*
Has mentioned it,
    Has mentioned it,   *night!*
So I carry the
    So I carry the
Knowledge
    Knowledge
Alone
    Alone
In these lines.
    In these lines.
Adelle would have reacted
    Adelle would have reacted   *the strangeness*
With a slight shudder.
    With a slight shudder.   *of an anniversary*

She didn't want people to know
She didn't want people to know   *without*
How long we'd been married
How long we'd been married   *you*
Because they always reacted
Because they always reacted
Strongly
Strongly
And because it
And because it
Dated her.
Dated her.
But I guess it's all right to say it
But I guess it's all right to say it
Now
Now
That she is timeless
That she is timeless
And can't hear
And can't hear
Either their exclamations
Either their exclamations
Or my
Or my
Scarcely hidden
Scarcely hidden

Pride.
Pride.

*

We met
We met
when we were twenty.
when we were twenty.
The sense
The sense
that I was given a life to care for.
that I was given a life to care for.
Did I care for it well?
Did I care for it well?
I hope so.
I hope so.
Did I cherish it properly
Did I cherish it properly
and help it to grow?
and help it to grow?
I hope so with all my heart
I hope so with all my heart
though there was never the sense
though there was never the sense
that the life would end
that the life would end
not even on that last
not even on that last

sad

    sad

day

    day

when you were alive and yourself in the morning

and by afternoon,

    and by afternoon,

gone,

    gone,

the life I was given

    the life I was given

having slipped away from

    having slipped away from

anything I

    anything I

could do

    could do

to save it.

    to save it.

Goodbye, love.

    Goodbye, love.

Tears every day

    Tears every day

for your sweet, intelligent, loving spirit.

    for your sweet, intelligent, loving spirit.

＊

dearest,

I'm so glad we had a child together.

December 31, 2016

＊

I relive your dying every day.

＊

From Carol Criss, a friend: *You deserve a good year.*

Jack: Thanks, Carol. Since 2016 contained what was unquestionably the worst day of my life—the day Adelle died—I figure that 2017 has to be better. And I'm doing all right. I have books—new books out recently and another on deck—projects, friends, family, publication, financial security, a radio show, listeners, people saying nice things about my work. But I carry my heart on my sleeve, and I cry on a dime. Every day, for a few moments at least, I re-experience Adelle's dying—and talk to her, as if talking to her were still possible.

For me, it isn't just the death: I saw Adelle *through* her death, was with her throughout. That experience is traumatizing, difficult to deal with. It keeps coming up on me, over and over.

For me, the problem of grief is the simultaneous presence and absence of the loved one—both experienced extremely intensely. It's what psychoanalysis calls a double bind. Probably the intensity will dim, but in some ways I don't want it to: the meltdowns bring her back to me vividly—so I want them, despite the fact that they are debilitating and remind me of her death. They are a link to her I still have; I don't want to lose it.

You exist now in vivid absence.

※

TO AN AUTHOR who wants me to do a show with him:

Yes, I would like to do a show with you, but I do have a problem. My usual procedure has been to read someone's book and discuss it with him/her. I have a capacity for empathy, and that has held me in good stead in these encounters. Since my wife's death, that capacity for empathy has diminished to some degree. I can enjoy someone else's work, but the ability to maintain a sustained discussion about it seems to have lessened considerably. I hope that this condition is not permanent but it is certainly real at the moment. Grief seems to have driven me into a kind of egotism.

What I have been doing in response to this situation is to have someone come over: we *both* present work, discuss poetry. Not so much an interview as such but a sharing of work—though of course I will ask some questions during the discussion.

If you are all right with this kind of presentation, we can do a show.

※

MELTDOWNS CONTINUE DAILY though perhaps I speak of them less. I'm at the Black Panther exhibit in Oakland. Fighting back tears because it reminds me so much of my early life with Adelle, discussions we had, etc. Grief is not something you get over. It becomes a part of your life, your history. This doesn't mean I can no longer experience joy.

*

they die

don't tell me about it

enemies & friends

I don't want to hear this

the ones around you

this is morbid

no one tells you

I want you to emphasize

when they wish "long life"

life

that not everyone has it

how nice it is

that people don't die together

to have friends

but piecemeal

to have lovers

some today

how good the taste

some yesterday

of ice cream &

some tomorrow

hamburgers

room for sorrow
  of Vietnamese
room for cessation
  pho
of anger
  stop with the whining
room in all of this
  grow up
for love
  you have plenty to live for
(sometimes)
  you have money
death
  friends
the great
  projects
contradictory
  why complain
force
  be
in
  positive
the
  love life
room

※

Dear Jack,

Thank you for your Xmas card which arrived today. But someone needs to say something to you, so I will reluctantly accept the responsibility.

You must stop burdening your friends with your seemingly unebbing grief over Adele (sic). We all have our sorrows to bear, but it is unfair for us to over-share our feelings. Many of us have losses we find it difficult to accept, but we must.

Love,

I answered:

> I'll do what I can in that direction, but we can only write what we're given to write.
>
> If you don't want to read what I write about Adelle (note the two l's), I'll take you off my list. I realize that there are things people repress, don't want to hear about.
>
> This morning, in addition to your note, I received this from another friend: "Good morning Jack, my wife and I both thank you profusely for the best written and most moving Christmas card we've ever gotten!"
>
> Different strokes for different folks. No pun required.

✳

I'd have gladly given my life for hers
If that would have made any difference.
No, said Death, I'll take both of you
But not at the same time.

For the Birthday of my Daughter in Law, Kerry, 2017

What do you do
When you look in your address book
And half your friends are dead?
Look to the living!
I am so glad
You are in my life
As I see the love you have
For my dear son—
In some ways
A mirror of the love I felt
For his mother,
My life-companion.
I have never believed in "marriage"—
A con by the state to control—
But I do believe in what Ezra Pound called
"The quality of the affection":
"Nothing matters," Pound wrote, "but the quality of the af-
        fection."
The love you feel for each other
Is what matters.
Whatever errors I have made in my son's upbringing
(And they are probably many)
It cheers me inestimably

To see in him
The capacity for love and sweetness,
And to see that capacity
Matched by your own.
Your parents perhaps
Felt that way about each other.
Sean could see
What Adelle and I could feel
Deeply about each other—
Whatever arguments we had,
Whatever collisions we engaged in.
I told her, shortly before her death,
"Don't let anyone tell you
We don't know how to do a marriage."
Dear Kerry,
My heart leaps to see
That you and Sean
Know how to do that too.
For me,
It is a gift beyond giving.

From 2013: A Birthday Poem For Sean @ 39

"The days of our years are threescore years and ten; and if by reason of
strength they be fourscore years, yet is their strength labour and sorrow;
for it is soon cut off, and we fly away."

—Psalm 90:10

39
Touches the line.
39 steps to what?
The old radio comedian
Jack Benny
Used to answer "39"
Whenever he was asked his age.
Everyone believed
He was lying:
39 is the edge
Of "middle age"
Which supposedly begins
At 40—
Past the half-way point
Of the Biblical "three score years and ten,"
But not quite "middle."
Besides, as you pointed out to me once,
We live longer these days.
Still, not being 40 *yet*

Still means something.
You have accomplished so much
That I begin to think I must have been prophetic
When—answering your childish request—I called you *astronaut*.
Time arcs and ranges.
You are something now:
You will be more.
Life falls around you like moonlight
On a clear night.
It beckons you to *do*.
At 72, I look back
At all the ache of time
And think of you
Like me, a man
In whom thought rages,
In whom there is little difference
Between "desire" and "intellect."
I was happy when you were born
All those years ago.
I'm happy now
To see the man you have become.
Whatever wisdom I have—
But I don't believe in "wisdom"—
Is yours for the asking.
We talk of Life
And all its worrisome mendacities

And triumphs
And tell each other

Stories

Full

Of laughter.

Added in 2017:

At 43
And 76
We pick up
The pieces
Of our lives
And see
What sticks.

✳

To my doctor:

I'm doing all right—thank you for asking. There are still tears every day, reminders. I call such moments "meltdowns," and there are often quite a few of them. They are debilitating—you can't do anything when they come—but they are also desired because, in a sense, they bring me closer to her: during a meltdown I can speak to her. In a sense, I relive her dying every day. When I'm not in meltdown mode, I'm fine and functional. The meltdowns keep me close to her despite her death. Since I'm a writer, words offer comfort and release, whether the words are specifically about Adelle or about other matters: writing is in fact my main source of comfort, but it is a powerful and deeply engaging source of comfort; I can pour my love and my grief into it, and there is always room left over...

I have been experiencing deep grief but I'm not sure I'm exactly "coming out" of it. It's possible that you don't come out of grief: rather, that grief enters into you, becomes a part of your history.

A FRIEND PHONED to tell me she had a dream—a visitation from Adelle. She said Adelle had given her a special message, something only Adelle and I knew, so I would know the visitation was real—except that the friend couldn't remember what the message was! The main thing, she said, was that Adelle is with me all the time and I can talk to her. "She was such a wonderful person. I wish you could have seen her." People tell you such things to comfort you, but their story is not about you or about the dead person: it is about them. Do they know how much pain their babble—their narcissistic projection—causes? How much you wish that it were true?

The March 1/21/17

for Adelle

You would have loved it!
Dell Dell would have loved it!
Imagination's camera pictures you
And all the Dellwackians
Emerging from lines on paper
Into the world
The EEE Monster
Dell Dell Dog (AHF!)
Dell Dell Biwd (CHIWP!)
Della Della Puella Bella
Old Woppa
Nuwse Nightindell
The Fleuws
Looney
All marching with the women
Who marched yesterday
If I close my eyes
I see them (and hear them)
A whirlpool a heartstorm of love
Thousands of them
And the Dellwackian males too
Jack Wack

The DDD Monster
Dw Quack
Salvador Dully
All linked to their mates
All singing
All flying in the face of.
They are dancing,
Dearest,
They are dancing.
They are all
Free

dearest, if there's a heaven
(in which I don't believe)
may you be in it

and may I see you again.

though I have seen your body
enter the fire,

may I see you again

Breakfast at Maliki restaurant in Oakland, January 2, 2016.

Jack and Adelle in Dubai, December 2013.

ADELLE JOAN FOLEY (August 15, 1940 – June 27, 2016) was a poet, a social, neighborhood and arts activist, and, for the past twenty years, a member of the administration of AC Transit. She was, in addition, a devoted and loving mother to her son, Sean Foley, and a deep friend to her daughter-in-law, Kerry. She married poet Jack Foley on December 21, 1961 (the longest night of the year), and their marriage was a long and happy one. The Foleys were familiar and much-loved figures in the local poetry scene, performing duets of Jack's unique choral pieces and Adelle's haiku. Beat poet Michael McClure wrote, "Adelle Foley's haikus show us humanity. Their vitality and imagination shine from her compassion; from seeing things as they truly are." Jack writes of "Your presence next to me as we read poetry together… your voice rising to mine."

Adelle was born in New York City to a dentist father and a mother who was both a housewife and a social activist, believing in liberal causes and active in The New York Herald Tribune Fresh Air Fund, an organization that provides free summer vacations in the country to New York City children from low-income families. Adelle continued her mother's activism in Oakland as a member of many local organizations, assisting in neighborhood clean ups, neighborhood watch programs, and in revitalizing the Melrose Branch of the Oakland Library in East Oakland. "Could they ever guess / that we'd be celebrating / in 2016?" she wrote for the Melrose Branch's centennial. She also worked for the City of Oakland, at one point chairing its Budget Advisory Committee. For these activities she was designated a "Local Hero." She was also a founding member of PEN Oakland and a member of the Board of the long-standing poetry organization, Poetry Flash.

Adelle graduated Phi Beta Kappa from Goucher College in 1961 and earned an MA in Economics from Cornell University in 1962. In 1963, she and Jack crossed the country in their 1956 Oldsmobile to Northern California, where they lived for the rest of their lives, settling for the first year in Berkeley and then in Oakland. Jack entered the University of California, Berkeley, as a graduate student in English literature, and Adelle found employment at the Federal Reserve Bank of San Francisco. She left the Fed in the early 1990s to work for the City of San Francisco and then, after a period of uncertainty, transitioned to AC Transit, first as a temp employee in 1993 and then full time in 1995. She enjoyed her work there, spending her final years with the company as Retirement Administrator.

In 1989, she began to write poetry. Her chosen form was haiku, which she wrote in the traditional 5-7-5 syllables. One of her most memorable, "Learning to Shave: Father Teaching Son," concerned her son, Sean, born in 1974: "A nick on the jaw / The razor's edge of manhood / Along the bloodline." Her book, *Along the Bloodline*, appeared in 2003. In it she declared, "It's not that I write / Because of what I see. I / See because I write." A second book, *Fennel in the Rain*—a collaboration with Jack—appeared in 2007. A final collection, edited by Jack, is forthcoming. The 2007 anthology, *For New Orleans*, featured Adelle's contribution on its cover, and her long-running column in "The MacArthur Metro" always concluded with a haiku.

Adelle Foley is remembered for her great intelligence, her quick wit, her sudden lyricism, her social conscience, and her flashing smile. She wrote in a "selfie" haiku: "An infectious smile / Tapping out daily Haiku / Pretty good figure."

In 1960 she sang an ancient French song, "A la Claire Fontaine," to Jack. The refrain of the song is "Il y a longtemps que je t'aime / Jamais je ne t'oublierai" ("I have loved you for a long time / I will never forget you"). Over the years they often sang the song together. In 2016 Jack sang the song to Adelle as she lay dying in the hospital: "I have loved you for a long time / I will never forget you."

Jack and Adelle Foley can be seen in many clips on YouTube.

Statement for the Inauguration of the Annual Adelle Foley Award From PEN Oakland

The annual Adelle Foley Award is given to a work, not fiction or poetry, that has done much to improve the relations between people in American society. The award honors my late wife Adelle and so, indirectly, honors me as well. I'd like to express my deep gratitude to PEN Oakland for creating this award. I can't imagine anything more needed at the moment than an improvement in the relations between people in American society.

Adelle Joan Foley, born August 15, 1940, died June 27, 2016, was a poet, a social, neighborhood and arts activist, and, for the past twenty years, a member of the administration of AC Transit. She was, in addition, a devoted and loving mother to her son, Sean Foley, and a deep friend to her daughter-in-law, Kerry.

Adelle and I were married on December 21, 1961 (the longest night of the year), and our marriage was a long and happy one. We became familiar figures in the local poetry scene, performing duets of my choral pieces and Adelle's haiku. Beat poet Michael McClure wrote, "Adelle Foley's haikus show us humanity. Their vitality and imagination shine from her compassion; from seeing things as they truly are." I wrote of her "presence next to me as we read poetry together…your voice rising to mine."

Adelle was born in New York City to a dentist father who frequently offered his services for free to the disadvantaged. He was called by a friend "the only poor dentist in New York." Adelle's mother was both a housewife and a social activist, believing in liberal causes and active in The New York Herald Tribune Fresh Air Fund, an organization that provides free summer vacations in the country to New York City children from low-income families. Adelle continued her mother's activism in Oakland as a member of many local organizations, assisting in neighborhood clean ups, neighborhood watch programs, and in revitalizing the Melrose Branch of the Oakland Library in East Oakland. "Could they ever guess / that we'd be celebrating / in 2016?" she wrote for the Melrose Branch's centennial. For these activities she was designated a "Local Hero." She was also a founding member of PEN Oakland and a member of the Board of the long-standing poetry organization, *Poetry Flash*.

Adelle graduated Phi Beta Kappa from Goucher College in 1961 and earned an MA in Economics from Cornell University in 1962. In 1963, she and I crossed the country in our 1956 Oldsmobile to Northern California, where we lived for the rest of our lives, settling for the first year in Berkeley and then in Oakland. I entered the University of California, Berkeley, as a graduate student in English literature, and Adelle found employment at the Federal Reserve Bank of San Francisco. Interestingly, she found this employment through the recommendation of the radical economist, Douglas Fitzgerald Dowd, with whom she had studied at Cornell. We were amused to note that Douglas Dowd had connections in the Capitalist sector. Adelle left the Fed in the early 1990s to work for the City of San Francisco and then, after a period of uncertainty, transitioned to AC Transit, first as a temp employee in 1993 and then full time in 1995. She enjoyed her work there, spending her final years with the company as Retirement Administrator. The post was a good one for her and provided her with an opportunity to employ her considerable intellect—she was a whiz at numbers—with the deep sense of compassion and empathy that I witnessed many times over. Hearing of her death, an African-American neighbor expressed his sorrow and told me, "She was the first person to welcome me to the neighborhood."

In 1989, Adelle began to write poetry. Her chosen form was haiku, which she wrote in the traditional 5-7-5 syllables. One of her most memorable, "Learning to Shave: Father Teaching Son," concerned our son, Sean, born in 1974:

> A nick on the jaw
> The razor's edge of manhood
> Along the bloodline.

Her book, *Along the Bloodline*, appeared in 2003. In it she declared,

> It's not that I write
> Because of what I see. I
> See because I write.

A second book, *Fennel in the Rain*—a collaboration with me— appeared in 2007. A final collection, which I'm editing, is forthcoming. Its title is *Early the Next Day*. The 2007 anthology, *For New Orleans*, featured Adelle's contribution on its cover, and her long-running column in the neighborhood newspaper, *The MacArthur Metro*, always concluded with a haiku.

Adelle Foley is remembered for her great intelligence, her quick wit, her sudden lyricism, her social conscience, and her flashing smile. She wrote—modestly—in a "selfie" haiku:

> An infectious smile
> Tapping out daily Haiku
> Pretty good figure.

The woman I knew—who had a *very* good figure—was far more than that. The response to her death has been extraordinary. I can only wish that she could have seen it. People from AC Transit, people from the poetry community, people from the neighborhood have all hastened to express their sorrow. There have been many poems. The response to her death has shown how many people—and how many *kinds* of people—she touched in her life. Recently a woman driving by stopped her car when she saw me. She told me she worked at AC Transit and had known Adelle: she said how kind Adelle had been, how smart she was. The woman had probably never read a line of Adelle's poetry. The California Buckeye planted in Oakland's Maxwell Park testifies to Adelle's extraordinary involvement in the neighborhood, in neighborhood projects. As I have said often, she had great intelligence, but she also had great compassion, a talent for empathy. For my whole life long, she made it possible for me to function as the kind of poet I am, and she believed in me as a poet when absolutely no one else did. I think she was happier about "Jack Foley Day" in Berkeley than I was because it justified the faith she had in me. And I'm sure she knew that the day honored her as much as it did me.

Her spirit enters into every young girl who has been fascinated by numbers and believes that she can handle money; into every person who believes that people have to *prove* themselves to be evil before you judge them so; into every cause that celebrates life, freedom, passion, and humor. She brought her beloved numbers into her poetry. I told her, "You like that form because it lets you count." In a performance with me, she tap danced on a dark stage whose boundaries she could not see.

I came upon this poem recently in a pile of papers that was devoted to things quite different from poetry. As it happened, the poem appeared to me on Adelle's birthday, August 15th. I think its sentiment is something we can carry in our hearts even in these dark times:

> The wind swirls around
> The pear tree. The branches bend
> But they do not break.

*

JAKE BERRY WRITES:

Empathy seems to fail. One has empathy with another. What you are dealing with is the loss of a self. That is why it has been so difficult. If marriage is the union of two people you and Adelle certainly had that and still do. That marriage is now the union of two worlds that we assume are opposite—though they obviously are not.

You have found a way to make something out of it. To carry the loss with you, but to continue. Nervous breakdown. How could it be anything else? The neurons that validated reality have been thrown into collapse by this absence. Reality changes. It always has, just not so violently. I remember a book you sent me once. It still sits on the shelf among my favorite spiritual books, called *Walker Between Worlds*. You are now precisely that. What *Grief Songs* affirms is that you can walk between those worlds and make a song of it—a dirge—but one full of vitality and intelligence.

Addendum: Poems for Adelle

Clara Hsu wrote this while Adelle was still alive though very sick. There are birds of paradise near our front door:

> ### for Adelle
>
> birds of paradise
> harbingers of good fortune
> endless love is now

A NUMBER OF POEMS were written for Adelle after her death, some by people who had never written a poem before.

Seeing photos from the mortuary, poet Lucille Lang Day wrote this:

> "Jack, these photos are heartbreaking, but yes, something of Adelle is still there. The photo of her hands is beautiful and lifelike. Their position says peace; the ring says love."

Later, Lucy wrote this poem:

Hands

For Adelle

Give me a hand, we say,
hoping someone will hold out one of those
prehensile, multi-fingered organs
found at the end of the forearm.

A koala hand has two opposable thumbs,
a raccoon hand doesn't have any,
a primate hand one. Like apes,
chimpanzees, monkeys
and lemurs, we also have
fingerprints to prove our touch
and fingernails instead of claws.

A human hand has twenty-seven bones.
The glabrous skin of the palm is thick
and lacking in melanin,
which makes palms more pale
than the rest of the body.

Lovers walk hand in hand
through city streets and in parks
where checkerspot butterflies
with black-and-orange wings
light on flowers.

If you're handy, you can fix
things with your hands.
We shake hands in greeting,
hold up our hands to surrender,
place a ring on another's hand
to signify commitment.

The last time I saw you,
the wedding ring you'd worn
for fifty-five years still shone
as you lay on white satin, your hands
resting on your paisley shawl
and purple shirt, the left on the right,
still uniquely your own
in this final pose,
and unexpectedly lovely.

My dear friend Ivan Argüelles read this at the funeral:

> Did I ever really know Adelle? I was initially intro-
> duced to her as Jack's partner in the recital of his fa-
> mous choruses, such as the Hummingbird chorus. Her
> voice was ringingly powerful, easily the match of Jack's
> poetic thunder. And she could modulate that voice in
> all the emotional registers necessary. But as for the
> real Adelle... I recall her pragmatic manner guiding
> us through the unknown streets of downtown Miami,
> one hot muggy tropical night punctuated by the sounds
> of contending salsa bands... or not too long ago going
> across the new Bay Bridge with Jack, we listened the
> three of us to a recording of Anton Karas playing on
> the zither the Theme from *The Third Man*, each note
> of that wonderful piece seemed to unite us in an enig-
> matic harmony... and our discussion of the movie it-
> self one of our favorites... But Adelle had the greatest
> effect on me with her sudden and fulminating death,
> which came all too swiftly... Jack had kept me up to
> date with reports of her terribly declining health from
> about mid-May... who could have expected this? Her
> death opened up with terrible clarity the Great Mys-
> tery for all of us.

Ivan wrote this on the day of Adelle's death:

WHEN THE HAND YOU HOLD
OF THE ONE YOU LOVE
SUDDENLY BECOMES
ALL OF SPACE

Adelle Foley, R.I.P.

who can know what the soul is
either a swarm of bees
clustering in the meadow of a noon
light honey and green fragrance
or the place smoke goes when
sky fades at the end of day
try as one might to understand the body
what is it but the infirmity of mind
to hold on to a name
yesterday is all of eternity
small voices ringing in unseen bells
calling back always calling back
what does it mean to *adumbrate?*
to cast a shadow on disappearing waves
to merge unconsciousness
with the shape of something passing
like a flower in a distant field

✳

OUR SON SEAN and our daughter in law Kerry were both moved to verse and wrote haiku in Adelle's 5-7-5 style. Kerry wrote a Beignet Haiku:

> Christmas in Oakland
> Mix, cut, fry dough, add sugar
> The beignet team's work

And Sean wrote a Giants Haiku:

> Two seats at the Stick
> Giants win in '89
> Shared love of baseball

※

Neeli Cherkovski, in Europe, wrote:

Hello Adelle

I see you are
Walking
Where no one has
Walked before, your clouds
Are made of
Glass, the roads all lead
To this solitude
No one else may entertain
The sun is made
Of mirrors, and the zoo
Is filled with wild
Women and wild men
And you are calm
In the center
Of the wilderness
Filled with appointments
And rooms of
Manuscripts and
Radio transcripts
It seems to be a space

No one has seen

Before, a secret door

Through walls of pain

Down here

At lakeside

The Italian lady

Says good morning

On Como's window

And I smile

Because your familiar voice

Travels through me

Like the morning butterfly

Long ago

Wearing lace

Woven by nuns

In their walled palace

Adelle at Thanksgiving

And at Christmas

And in a restaurant

Adelle and Jack

Jack in his song

Adelle at home

Up a flight of language

Here comes Adelle

And everybody

Though she steps

Into the secret of
Her magic words
That she may find
Her name
Forged on the doorpost
And in the enduring
Light at the end
Of all our days

＊

AL YOUNG WROTE a poem for Adelle's birthday:

For Whom the Bells Toll

They toll and ring for you alone
this time around, Adelle Foley.
In the Holy Poetry City we share,
Bells toll strong. You stare back
at Jack and me. Comfortable.
Wonderful. You died to set each
lasting one of us free, a living pittance
Each one of us, yes, dear one, free
as free a peach as poetry. Bitten
into, salt-sprinkled, lime sprinkled,
all of you all Jack needs. Toll. Toll on.
HAPPY BIRTHDAY, ADELLE FOLEY

※

CHRISTOPHER BERNARD WROTE the elegiac "Words for Adelle":

Welcome silence.
Ours is one thing only: this
singing momentariness.
Welcome nothingness.
Welcome darkness.
Timelessness out of time,
life looking for its rhyme.
Welcome sleep.
Welcome quiet.
Out of the shabby thing called life,
human strife, its helplessness,
will-o'-wisp and hollow pride,
space and time, their emptiness,
broken bodies, vanishing minds,
flash of singing, worlds, breath.
Welcome stillness.

＊

Our friend Rosetta Egan wrote this for the memorial:

> After my daughter was murdered I became very ill. You came to my house and I'd cook pasta or we had tea and watched movies, talked about neighborhood issues like traffic or just about the movie or TV show we watched. You offered to pick me up to go to neighborhood meetings. This really helped me to stay connected with the community at a time when I could have retreated into sadness and grief. You were a quiet leader with a warm generous smile as well as a talented poet and good at Sudoku. I admired and respected your commitment to our community, which you demonstrated by your cheerful presence at neighborhood meetings and clean-ups. I began to feel happiness again and enjoyed immensely the times I spent with you and Jack, another wonderful kind talented person as well. You added a dimension to my life, enriching it and I've learned so much from both of you.
>
> Thank you for being a friend to me.
>
> Thank you both.

KATHERINE HASTINGS WROTE:

Adelle's Haiku

In Sweet Memory

How we heard of cats
beneath *Beware of Dog* signs
Oakland in three lines.
Newspapers wrote *Death*
in Oakland. Adelle wrote *Life*.
Train whistles, light, love
corn-rowed on BART or
wandering among sea gull wings
off in the distance

July 12, 2016

※

Mary-Marcia Casoly wrote:

Haiku Bird Has Flown

rendering a space
no more than three lines empty
large expanding bright
such a solo performance
has never been so

so enormous, gone.
Her presence always being
just right, skillfully,
steeping herself, pouring
tea into our cups.

What a good friendship
when her eyes met yours offering
a quick nod, smart smile
she understood your problems.
And then the charm of

her voice, rising in duet
meeting the demand
then, after words performance,
subduing her silks
for tall tales of literature

Jack-in-the-bean talk
Who was the charm of her life?
    What was the charm of her life?
Steady in the back-
ground counting on change, counting
syllables count-count

The egrets are back,
Oakland sightings, reporting
her marvels, we'll miss
her, those talks of tea, beignet.

Haiku bird flown, gone humming-
bird beyond every

＊

AND JAKE BERRY wrote "Evocations for Adelle," a long, gorgeous poem which brought Adelle and our life together back to me most vividly. It ends,

> I remember your face
>> as if I am seeing it for the first time—
> I am falling in love with you
>> so suddenly, I am drowning in forever.
> How many of us?
>> So many I cannot see them all—
>> The family we carry in our blood—
>> Our son, trembling in my arms—
>> I have waited so long to see you!
>> "A child of Earth and starry Sky."
>
>> a razor
>>> "a nick on the jaw"
>>> a day the same unlike any other
>>> "along the bloodline"
>
> I remember the rituals we kept—
>> our private rites
>>> held toward the sky inside
> I repeat each one step by step
> I know this dance so well,

so completely that I forget myself
    I forget my self
    as if the last step
    is a light beyond Earth, sun and starry sky—

Remember, child, remember—
Drink deeply—
    the water over your head
    drowning forever in love
    You have come into being

"a haze—nirwanna—rest and night—oblivion."

    The fresh wet light
    The rain's sweet music

    Remember
With you now, my love,
the multitude born in us
remembering, remembering!
    gone out
    in waves
    unbound!

Nothing born of starlight knows this embrace.

    The oblivion of your kiss.
    The fresh wet light

THE LIGHT THAT PASSES
IN THE SWEETNESS OF SORROW
THROUGH A BLADE OF GRASS
THE GRASS SEEMS DARKER;
IS THE SOUL THAT DISAPPEARS
THE SOUL APPEARS
BEFORE NIGHT FALLS
IN THE TANGLE OF ROOTS

can never have back the substance
her body
that used to fit all these clothes
now a flame
the matter suffused with heat
cooled;
nerve and pulsing veins
her voice
it used to talk and move heights
in the air, my dreams,
wander air and earth afar
on the internet,
mobility of love passion stained
sings
nights like cities full of mystery
to my waiting,

remembering this

Be still a moment—
Can you hear
in this silence

the boundless water
calling?

FINALLY, GAIL MITCHELL:

It is in the longing and the turning again and again
the seasons make sense the rocks pebbles and sacred awe
of breath it is the comings and going and tears that
show me self worth is not quantifiable Joy begets Joy
and the smell of sandalwood, frangipani and patchouli
remind that all is holy.

IVAN ARGÜELLES WROTE a poem not for Adelle but fo

THE LIGHT THAT PASSES THROUGH A BLADE OF GRA IS THE SOUL THAT DISAPPE BEFORE NIGHT FALLS

for Jack Foley

can never have back the substance
that used to fit all these clothes
the matter suffused with heat
nerve and pulsing veins
it used to talk and move heights
wander air and earth afar —
mobility of love passion stained
nights like cities full of mystery
simply going out into the dawn
white evanescent imperturbable

August 26, 2016

I answered it with a writing between the lines:

simply going out into the dawn
    dying
white evanescent imperturbable
      heart

A Gaggle of Poems in Epilogue

Afterglow

(my translation of a poem by Jorge Luis Borges: Borges's title is in English)

AFTERGLOW

Siempre es conmovedor el ocaso
por indigente o charro que sea,
pero más conmovedor todavía
es aquel brillo desesperado y final
que herrumbra la llanura
cuando el sol último se ha hundido.
Nos duele sostener esa luz tirante y distinta,
esa alucinación que impone al espacio
el unánime miedo de la sombra
y que cesa de golpe
cuando notamos su falsía,
como cesan los sueños
cuando sabemos que soñamos.

AFTERGLOW

Sunset always moves us,
Sunset always moves us,

whether it is gaudy or impoverished,

whether it is gaudy or impoverished,

but even more moving

but even more moving

is that last luminosity, desperate and final,

is that last luminosity, desperate and final,

that turns the plain to the color of rust

that turns the plain to the color of rust

when the sun has finally

when the sun has finally

gone down.

gone down.

We have trouble enduring that tense, distinct light,

We have trouble enduring that tense, distinct light,

that hallucination which imposes on space

that hallucination which imposes on space

the unanimous human fear of shadows—

the unanimous human fear of shadows—

and which stops suddenly

and which stops suddenly

when we see its falseness,

when we see its falseness,

as dreams end

as dreams end

when we know we are dreaming.

when we know we are dreaming.

For James Joyce's Birthday (Feb 2)

Is it yer birthday is it, says I. Yes, it is, says me. Well if it's yr
birthday what do ye do with the thingamajig? says I. You mean
the fact that I've been dead for a good many years now? says me.
I do indead, says I. Well, it's true that I am among the not so
recently decessed, yssss, that's true. But I don't decay, you know,
says me. What do you mean you don't decay? says I. I stopped
being a man but I became something else, says me. And what is
that, pray? says I. It's a book, says me. All lion hearts are Catlick
in the tomb. And we Rise awake when you shake a page. When
you shake a page, we rage. These pages are the leaves that grow
out of Yggdrasil, the dendritic centaurs branching out and out.
And when we fall we fly. Do we now? says I. Yes, says me, we
fly UP when we fall. Into the arms of Seamus O'Toole the great
Cocksman, who cockadoodle doos in the year of the Roister. Hear
his cry. And every cry is a birth of a baby and every baby is a dooer
and a door and every tear is a cry and every cry tears the heart till
it opens. And when it opens it's a birth and a bath of heartsblood.
O the Catlicks. We know it down to our paws. And our maws too,
if it comes to that. Well, says I, if you open your ma it's surely a
birth and the birth must be a day and the day is today in the vast
Fibruary in the great ocean of time on the second day in the year
of the Orange fool in the Great White House (where is the Green
where is the Green?). I'm with you there since how could we be
separate you and I? When I open the book I fall and it's Fall but

it's Winter and Spring too with snow falling like leaves like words like wonners that come with wings. And the dead spring up and sings: Ah, Blarney Castle, ah, drunkenness, ah, sweet irrevocables and vocables, and we wing it as the day moves on and the night (ah, night) falls too.

They Die (Repeated Here)

they die
don't tell me about it
enemies & friends
I don't want to hear this
the ones around you
this is morbid
no one tells you
I want you to emphasize
when they wish "long life"
life
that not everyone has it
how nice it is
that people don't die together
to have friends
but piecemeal
to have lovers
some today
how good the taste
some yesterday
of ice cream &
some tomorrow
hamburgers
room for sorrow
of Vietnamese

room for cessation
pho
of anger
stop with the whining
room in all of this
grow up
for love
you have plenty to live for
(sometimes)
you have money
death
friends
the great
projects
contradictory
why complain
force
be
in
positive
the
love life
room

For Mary-Marcia Casoly

Death
Comes to your birth-
Day this year,
Telling his weary
Tale,
Reminding you
Of loss, loss, loss
Now and in the past,
Your brother's
Spirit
No longer in the world.
We all
Experience loss
But the closeness here
Is especially painful,
As are
The dread legalities
That follow
A dying.
What can we birth today?
An absence, an abyss
Colors everything.
Grief
Is the simultaneous

Presence and
Absence
Of a loved one.
Yet birth remains,
In all the dark of dying,
A light, a hope, a promise.
Today's celebration
Revolves around candles,
Around flame,
Around emblems of the sun.
You see them, love them,
Blow them out
And move on.

For Anthony Holdsworth's Birthday 2017

rare is the painter who paints in the light
>   *rare is the painter who paints in the light*
of joy who paints with care in the clear
>   *of joy who paints with care in the clear*
light of day whose mind occupies itself
>   *light of day whose mind occupies itself*
with the rareness of
>   *with the rareness of*
the ordinary whose brush exposes the clear
>   *the ordinary whose brush exposes the clear*
chiaroscuro of being / the rare, clear light
>   *chiaroscuro of being / the rare, clear light*
that emanates from things that are
>   *that emanates from things that are*
radiant in the mind's gaze
>   *radiant in the mind's gaze*
in the gaze of an eye that dis-covers
>   *in the gaze of an eye that dis-covers*
love
>   *love*
in light
>   *in light*

For Sean on Mother's Day, 2017

There's a photo
Taken not too long ago
By you or Kerry
Of Adelle and me
Arriving at Dubai Airport.
You were greeting us,
"Picking us up at the airport"
I, bad back and all,
Was carrying luggage
And looking
None too happy about it.
Adelle saw you and flashed
Her marvelous smile.
Love
Poured out from her.
The joy
Of seeing you again
After a long absence.
A few years back,
She told me that I had been a good father
I told her that she had been a good mother
Narcissism
Is perhaps an element of all parental love
But if so it is a *good* narcissism
One that allows the parent to feel joy
At the child's successes
And sorrow at the child's failures.

Adelle loved you with enormous pride
But it was pride that had to answer
To the intelligence that steered her
Through every aspect of her world.
If you had not justified the pride
She would perhaps have felt it still
But with pain
And questioning whether
There were something more she might have done.
Such pain was never an aspect of her relationship to you.
She spoke of you with love
And pride that was justified by all you have accomplished
And by the love and intelligence
With which you react to the world.
I can feel that love now
Almost a year after her death
Informing everything she did for you.
It is still her day.
She will never cease to be your mother.
The love she felt
Is something you carry in your bones,
My dear son,
Something that fashioned you
After the nothing you were
When they took you out of her womb.
My son,
Her son,
Honored on her day.

Dream

In the dream,
In the dream,
I wake in the morning
I wake in the morning
Go to sleep at night
Go to sleep at night
Everything in between
Everything in between
Is simultaneously
Is simultaneously
Real and unreal.
Real and unreal.
I know it's a dream
I know it's a dream
But everything is substantial, real
But everything is substantial, real
I am playing
I am playing
In a movie of my life
In a movie of my life
Someone else
Someone else
Has written the plot
Has written the plot
And continuity
And continuity

But I am responsible
But I am responsible
For my lines
For my lines
Which I improvise.
Which I improvise
At will.
At will.
I talk
I talk
But it makes no difference
But it makes no difference
To the dream.
To the dream.
I wake
I wake
I sleep
I sleep
The waking
The waking
And the sleeping
And the sleeping

Are the dream
Are the dream
Too
Too

GREGORY VINCENT ST. THOMASINO sent me his poem, "Decoration Day" last year. I answered it with a writing between the lines. The paired poems were the last thing Adelle and I recorded. She read my lines and read them well, as she always did. The lines seem, now, oddly appropriate:

> We watch
> as the waters
>
> ebb, flow,
> return
>
> to ocean-
> home

I offer the poems here, for Memorial Day.

Decoration Day

> going, and sounding, how, gathering
> and again
>
> a putting into place, a following
> of similar. A
>
> turning back, to an end. In arrival
> or disposition

in measure, in picture
are several, having one, and, role

according, as, is an end.
As high is far or near, or, save to say

In such a case, are all, are, similar
Are all, are, an end

and so on. And ever so, to
part or like.

My writing between the lines:

Decoration Day

Memorial Day

going, and sounding, how, gathering
    the dead
and again
    gather in our minds

a putting into place, a following
    speaking
of similar. A
    a language we do not

turning back, to an end. In arrival
understand.
or disposition
we understand

in measure, in picture
measure, denial,
are several, having one, and, role
something common to the earth.

according, as, is an end.
We watch
As high is far or near, or, save to say
as the waters

In such a case, are all, are, similar
ebb, flow,
Are all, are, an end
return

and so on. And ever so, to
to ocean-
part or like.
home

May 29, 2017

Yahrzeit (June 27, 2017)

for Adelle

It is
What the Jews call Yahrzeit,
A year since your death.
The word stings.
If you retain any consciousness of the world
You know
That I have found a new love.
She has been
A wonder and a comfort
In my grief for you.
I think you would have liked her
(And mothered her!).
Going through your dresser drawer
As we attempt to find room for her things,
She found
A fancy, almost comically sexy garter.
I had forgotten it
But recognized it immediately.
You wore it only once,
On the night of December 21, 1961,
Our wedding night;
You kept it, as you kept many other things, for all these years.

How we formed each other.

How we treasured each other's hearts.

If the stories are true,

You may be in bliss

While I find my way through this quivering wall of sorrow
       and tears.

And love.

My first love, my dear first love,

It has been a year

(Has it been a year?),

Yahrzeit.

Your ashes

Remain   in the vanishing morning light.

JACK FOLEY (born 1940) has published thirteen books of poetry; five books of criticism; *The Tiger and Other Tales*, a book of stories; and *Visions and Affiliations*, a "chronoencyclopedia" of California poetry from 1940 to 2005. His radio show, *Cover to Cover,* is heard on Berkeley station KPFA every Wednesday at 3.

With his late wife, Adelle, Foley performed his work (often "multivoiced" pieces) frequently in the San Francisco Bay Area. He is continuing to work with others. With poet Clara Hsu, Foley is co-publisher of Poetry Hotel Press.

In 2010 Foley was awarded the Lifetime Achievement Award by the Berkeley Poetry Festival, and June 5, 2010 was proclaimed "Jack Foley Day" in Berkeley.